D0178097

GLORY DAYS

STEAM in DORSET

Michael H. C. Baker

MARINE AND MOTOR ENGINEERS

REPAIRERS AND CHANDLERS

HOSTEL FOR SEAME

Ian Allan
PUBLISHING

Front cover:
On 28 December 1965
BR Standard Class 4 2-6-4T
No 80039 departs from
Blandford with the
12.30pm Templecombe-
Bournemouth service.
Hugh Ballantyne

Back cover:
Within a few weeks of the
end of steam in Dorset BR
Standard Class 4 No 75076
heads an up train out of
Bournemouth Central on
15 June 1967. *R. C. Riley*

Title page:
No 1370, one of the
outside-cylinder 0-6-0
pannier tanks designed by
Collett in 1934, heads past
the hostel for seamen on
Weymouth Quay bound for
the Quay station, 31 May
1950. *J. C. Flemons*

CONTENTS

First published 1998

ISBN 0 7110 2610 6

© Michael Baker 1998

Published by Ian Allan Publishing

an imprint of Ian Allan Publishing Ltd, Terminal House, Station
Approach, Shepperton, Surrey TW17 8AS.
Printed by Ian Allan Printing Ltd, Riverdene Business Park,
Molesey Road, Hersham, Surrey KT12 4RG.

Code: 9811/B3

Gas lamps and semaphores
at Weymouth. Both survived
into the 1970s.
M. H. C. Baker

INTRODUCTION

Dorset is one of the most rural of all English counties. Which, of course, has conferred on it many advantages. It has never boasted any heavy industry to speak of, and not one mile of motorway can be found within its boundaries. However such a scenario does have its disadvantages, particularly for promoters and builders of railways.

Along with a lack of industry this essentially rural county has always been relatively sparsely populated. Since the mid-19th century most of its inhabitants have lived beside the sea and at the last count over a half of the total were in the conurbation of Poole, Bournemouth and Christchurch. Until the boundary changes of 1974 the two latter towns were in Hampshire. Many of their inhabitants joined Dorset only under protest and great was the rejoicing when Bournemouth, like Poole, became a unitary authority in April 1997, although they are still in Dorset. Only those wise and learned sages at Westminster who make such decisions can tell you why Christchurch should be left out on a far eastern limb, still not part of its beloved Hampshire but physically barely part of the county which controls its destiny.

For our purposes we will allow Bournemouth to be part

Pride of Weymouth shed, No 4080 *Powderham Castle* accelerates past Dorchester Junction, where the former Great Western and Southern routes meet, with a Paddington-Weymouth express in August 1951. *Dennis Morris*

A most unusual sight at Weymouth. Gresley streamliner 'A4' Pacific No 60024 *Kingfisher* heads an LCGB railtour out of Weymouth, passing the engine shed on its way to Waterloo, 25 March 1966.
Tony Trood

of Dorset, even though it was not in the days of steam. This is logical enough on several counts. One; Bournemouth West station was within sight of the pre-1974 boundary and many of its departures were headed straight for Dorset. Two; any pictures on the Hampshire side of the old boundary are of trains bound for, or coming from Dorset. Three; it enables us to include some excellent images of steam trains which we should otherwise have to leave out!

The rest of the world tends to have a somewhat romantic, 19th century view of life down in Dorset. The Wessex Electric which stands at Platform 9, 10 or 11 in Waterloo station is usually 10 coaches long. The first five coaches are for Bournemouth and if you get into these and move down them, you can always tell when you have reached the front five which are bound for Wareham, Wool, Dorchester and Weymouth, because many of the occupants wear smocks, have straw behind their ears and tend to intersperse much of their conversation with 'Oh, aahs', 'my luvvie', and such like. At least this is what sophisticated city and suburban types like to think.

Thomas Hardy is to blame for a lot of this. I kid you not. A few years ago my wife and two of her friends, headteachers and deputies, were attending an educational conference one Saturday in Bristol. The speaker in the morning was Professor Ted Wragg, quite the best informed and most entertaining man in the business, whom any sensible government would put in charge of the whole education caboodle. The afternoon session promised to be of rather lower quality and so the three of them decided to play truant, hailed a taxi, and headed for the bright lights of the city centre. Chattering away with excitement at being let loose (but only after one of them, now an inspector, had been accosted by another member of the conference as to where she was going and had grasped said member by the sleeve and whispered in her ear, 'If you split on us I'll take you behind the cycle sheds and duff you over.' – God's truth!) the taxi driver turned and asked where they were from. 'Dorset,' was the reply. Pause. 'Have you ever been to London?' he asked.

The main line from Waterloo to Weymouth had a long and interesting existence as a steam route; indeed it was billed at the end, in 1967, as the last steam-operated main line on British Rail. Until 1959 it had had a rival, the former Great Western line out of Paddington, but at the end of the summer timetable of that year it ceased to be a through route to and from London, and from then on the former London & South Western line had a monopoly.

It was the ports of Weymouth and Poole which had been the principal attractions for the 19th century railway promoters. Weymouth shared with Southampton the Channel Islands traffic, while Poole's chief business was in the coastal trade and fishing. Both desperately needed the boost of a direct rail link with London to revive their fortunes. Weymouth, following the opening of the London & Southampton Railway in 1841, had lost the Channel Islands Royal Mail contract to the Hampshire port, while Poole's Newfoundland trade, which had once made its merchants prosperous, was in terminal decline.

The two London to Weymouth lines dominate the story of Dorset's railways and it is easy to forget that a third

◄ A view of Dorchester South station taken from the steps of the signalbox on 27 August 1954. Easing its way round the curve opposite the down platform is Urie 'N15' 4-6-0 No 30739 *King Leodegrance* with the 2.20pm Weymouth to Andover stopping train, composed of a set of elderly LSWR non-corridors. *King Leodegrance* will back his train past the bogie goods brake van into the up dead-end platform on the right, a relic of the long-ago intention that this should form part of a through route to Exeter and the West of England. *R. C. Riley*

main line, that between London, Salisbury and Exeter, also passes through the county. But 'passes' is very much the operative word. Between Shaftesbury and Axminster it weaves its way in and out of the county and only three of its stations, Gillingham, Templecombe and Sherborne, are in Dorset. Others, such as Chard Junction, Crewkerne, Milborne Port and Semley, drew most of their business from north Dorset, while much of the network of lines, sidings and junctions between Yeovil Junction and Yeovil Pen Mill were in Dorset even if, strictly speaking, both stations belonged to Somerset.

Readers need hardly be reminded of the famous Somerset & Dorset – even if there are cynics who claim that its popularity today is in inverse ratio to the number of people who actually travelled on it – which ran roughly parallel to the Dorchester Yeovil line, while the third north to south route was the branch from Poole and Wimborne to Fordingbridge and Salisbury. There were seven other branch lines, all serving the seaside in one form or another. Most westerly was the Lyme Regis branch, which left the LSWR's West of England main line at Axminster and only

crossed the border from Devon into Dorset as it approached its terminus. Next came the GWR branch from Maiden Newton, between Dorchester and Yeovil, to Bridport and West Bay. Between Dorchester and Weymouth the GWR line to Abbotsbury branched off the main line at Upwey Junction.

The Portland branch, which did not quite pass through Weymouth station but took off beside it and headed over the inner reaches of the harbour for the Isle of Portland, was a joint GWR and LSWR operation. Much the most photographed (although the Lyme Regis branch ran it a fairly close second) was the Weymouth harbour line, stamping ground for a variety of small GWR tank engines.

Moving into LSWR territory, there was the Swanage branch which left the main line at Wareham. Finally there was the Hamworthy line, freight only for most of its existence, which branched off at Hamworthy Junction to its terminus on the edge of Poole Harbour.

Strictly speaking we should mention the military railway which served the still-extant army camp at Bovington. It branched off the main line at Wool. It

'M7' 0-4-4T No 106 leaving Broadstone with the 10.33am Hamworthy Junction-Wimborne stopping train composed of five LSWR carriages some time in the 1930s. The line in the foreground is the S&D line to Blandford and the north. *G. W. Puntis*

Wareham, 4 May 1966. On the left is the now-preserved 'Merchant Navy' No 35028 *Clan Line* with the 16.35 Waterloo-Weymouth, while on the right a grimy – although an attempt has been made to clear the rear section – BR Standard '4MT' 2-6-4T No 80065, minus numberplate, is ready to depart with the connecting 19.28 to Swanage. Standard 2-6-4Ts once again run to Swanage, although they do not yet connect at Wareham. *Tony Trood*

A Weymouth-Waterloo express ascending the 1 in 60 Parkstone Bank behind 'Merchant Navy' No 35026 *Lamport & Holt Line*, 10 June 1949. *H. Weston*

A most unusual visitor at Broadstone, *c*1938: GWR 'Saint' 4-6-0 No 2916 *Saint Benedict*, having arrived at Bournemouth with a train from Wolverhampton, has for some reason been sent to turn on the Holes Bay-Hamworthy Junction-Broadstone triangle. Perhaps the Bournemouth depot turntable was out of action. *G. W. Puntis*

opened on 9 August 1919 and closed less than 10 years later on 4 November 1928, and was never used by the general public. There was also a branch which served Blandford Camp, which opened in 1918 and closed for good in 1921.

So what do we have today; what is left 32 years after the last regular steam train ran on British Rail tracks in Dorset? The Weymouth line, although singled between Moreton and Dorchester, flourishes and was electrified in 1988. The old GWR main line between Castle Cary, Yeovil and Dorchester has also been singled and is now only a branch line, but it still provides a service to Bristol and South Wales. The LSWR main line from Waterloo to Exeter has been singled for much of its length west of Salisbury, the former GWR route to the West of England having gained the ascendancy. The Somerset & Dorset closed on

7 March 1966. Of the branch lines, that along the quay at Weymouth still exists, although it is a long time since it saw regular use. The Swanage branch closed in 1972, apart from the two-mile section to the clay works at Furzebrook, but it has been reopened stage by stage as far as Norden and will soon once again be complete. The Hamworthy branch still soldiers on, carrying a variety of freight from the docks. Preserved steam flourishes on the Swanage branch, much of it hauled by locomotives of a type long familiar in Dorset. On the main line an occasional steam special has reached Weymouth, from both the Yeovil and Bournemouth directions.

The 1.3pm Bournemouth West-Salisbury eases out of Parkstone behind Maunsell 'N' 2-6-0 No 31841, 31 March 1962.
Michael J. Fox

BR Standard '5MT' 4-6-0 No 73114 of Eastleigh depot, approaching Sherborne with an up stopping train, 8 November 1958. *B. A. Poley*

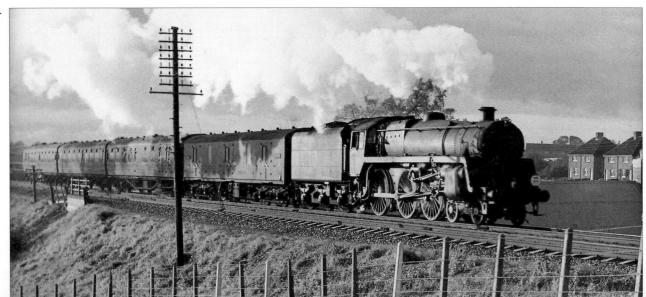

Much of the plot of the story of the early days of Dorset's railways is concerned with the rivalry between the London & South Western and the Great Western Railways. In some ways Dorset was only a bit player, the real object of both companies' desires being Exeter and the far west – Plymouth and Cornwall that is, not Atchison, Topeka and Santa Fé territory. It was only some 10 years ago that the most concrete – well, brick mostly – remnant of this feud was swept away when Dorchester South station was rebuilt. The LSWR had shuffled onto this mortal coil as the London & Southampton Railway on 12 May 1838. Just over a year later it signified its greater ambitions with its change of name. For some time it was uncertain whether Exeter would be reached by way of Salisbury, reached in June 1847, or Dorchester. In 1844 a Wimborne solicitor, Charles Castleman, proposed a line between Southampton and Dorchester. The LSWR was lukewarm in its support so the enterprising Castleman made overtures to the GWR, which had already reached Exeter. Ever anxious to contain their rivals' ambitions, the GWR board signed a provisional agreement with Castleman. Of course the GWR was at this time 100% broad gauge and so the Southampton to Dorchester line would be built to the 7ft gauge. It would connect with the Wiltshire, Somerset & Weymouth Railway which would branch off the London to Bristol main line. All of this was part of the grander politicking indulged in by the two rivals. A few months later other considerations led them to agree that the LSWR would operate the Southampton to Dorchester as a standard gauge route and that the GWR would continue on to Weymouth on the broad gauge.

Work on the Southampton & Dorchester Railway began in August 1845. The easiest way to bring in the various building materials was by sea and so Poole saw the first railway construction in Dorset. Poole station was not on the site of the one we know today but at the end of a one and three-quarter mile long branch line, at what has for

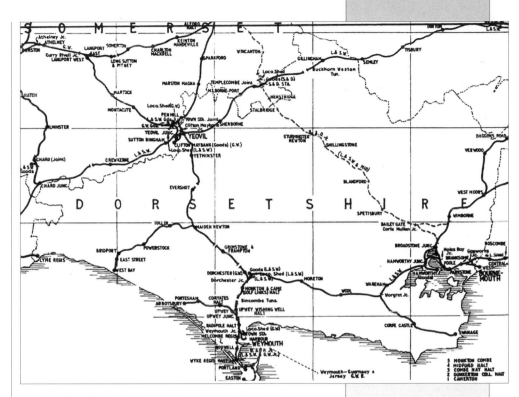

nearly all its life been known as Hamworthy Quay. The main line station was then called Poole Junction. The present Poole station site came into use on 2 December 1872 and was at the end of a branch line from Broadstone. Although part of an enterprise known as the Poole & Bournemouth Railway, there were as yet no trains running through to Bournemouth, the only ones being those on the Somerset & Dorset to Wimborne, Blandford Forum and points north.

The first section at the Dorset end of what would become the Somerset & Dorset, the Dorset Central, opened

Quintus, an 0-4-0ST built by Manning Wardle in 1914, at work on one of the narrow gauge lines which served the numerous clay mines on the Isle of Purbeck and which connected with the Swanage branch at Furzebrook, site of the present day oil and gas terminal, and at Norden, site of the present park and ride station, c1951. *Ivo Peters*

between Wimborne and Blandford Forum on 1 November 1860. There was infinitely more business carried on at sea around the British coastline in those days, and not only was it a very roundabout route from Bristol and north Somerset to the south coast by way of Land's End, it was also often hazardous with many shipwrecks all along the coast. Therefore the idea of carrying this traffic safely and quickly by rail resulted in a number of proposals to link the Bristol and English Channels. The first was achieved on 31 August 1863, when the line to Highbridge and Burnham-on-Sea was completed. The northern section had been built by a company known as the Somerset Central Railway. The two amalgamated on 1 September 1862 to become the Somerset & Dorset.

Both separately and together they held ambitions on Bristol – logically enough, for through travel, whether passenger or goods, from Burnham itself never amounted to very much. Various Great Western branches thwarted

this and it was the Midland Railway which provided the next best thing, when it reached Bath in 1869. The Somerset & Dorset set about building a costly 26-mile extension from Evercreech by way of four tunnels and a number of viaducts to Bath and the line opened on 20 July 1874. Right from the start through carriages from the Midlands, from Birmingham to be precise, were worked through to Poole and Bournemouth.

However, although traffic did increase, both passenger and goods, the company had got itself so deeply into debt that it could no longer carry on as an independent concern. Negotiations opened and it looked as though the GWR together with the Bristol & Exeter – these two were not yet one – and the LSWR would become joint owners. This would have been logical enough, but not as far as the LSWR was concerned. It co-operated with its traditional rival when it suited it, but Waterloo had no expectations of the GWR doing much to encourage through trade with the Somerset & Dorset, whereas the Midland Railway clearly would. So, before Paddington knew what was happening, a deal was signed for a 999-year lease from 1 November 1875 and the LSWR and the Midland Railway were now joint owners of the Somerset & Dorset.

We have jumped ahead of ourselves chronologically, and we must move backwards to record that the first public railway trains in Dorset, two down and one up, ran between Southampton, Ringwood, Wimborne, Poole Junction, Wareham and Dorchester on 1 June 1847. The tunnel passing under the centre of Southampton was not yet finished, but it was ready a couple of months later. With its opening Dorset was now on the direct line to London and it was possible to make the return journey between the capital and the Dorset county town in a single day, the fastest single journey taking five and a half hours. The effect was dramatic and the ripples of this transformation would reach out across the county. Even today there are parts which, superficially at least, seem little touched by 19th and 20th century developments but this is illusion, for the life of every single inhabitant was changed for ever the day those first three trains steamed between Southampton and Dorchester. The old master of rural doom and gloom, Thomas Hardy, recognised this, and the railway features in many of his stories and poems.

The original regular service consisted of five trains in each direction between Southampton and Dorchester, some of which continued to or from London, and four on Sundays. The locomotives which hauled these trains were 2-2-2s. Although the first Locomotive Superintendent was Joseph Woods, they were not designed by him, being more or less standard products of various builders. Woods had gone by the time the Dorset section of the LSWR was opened but the engines he ordered were a familiar sight there, although most had short lives, as was common at that time with technology moving at such a rapid rate. Goods engines were 0-4-2s.

Woods was succeeded by John Viret Gooch, brother of Swindon's celebrated Daniel, in 1843. Gooch continued with engines of the same wheel arrangement, but to his own designs. Some were ordered from outside builders, Rothwell and Fairburn for examples, but he also built his own at Nine Elms Works, which began to produce locomotives in the year Gooch took up his post. Both Woods and Gooch knew a good design when they saw one and the earliest London & Southampton and LSWR engines were much better than those found on many early railways. Two of the earliest Gooch express engines were called *Snake* and *Serpent*. Now the line between Southampton and Dorchester became known as the 'Snake' or 'Castleman's Corkscrew' on account of the

One of the Midland Railway '2P' 4-4-0s built for the S&D in 1914 approaching Broadstone with an express from the north, composed of LMS corridor stock; pictured around the time the LMS and SR assumed direct control of the line in 1930. *L&GRP*

roundabout route it followed; whether there was any connection between this and the names of those early Gooch engines is not recorded.

In 1844 Gooch brought out four heavy goods 0-6-0 engines which, to emphasise their amazing pulling powers, were called *Bison*, *Buffalo*, *Elephant*, and *Rhinoceros*. None of the early LSWR locomotives had numbers, although some lasted long enough to acquire them. An 0-6-0 may not seem very large by latter day standards but it remained more or less the norm for as long as steam existed in Dorset. 2-10-0s and 2-8-0s appeared on the Somerset & Dorset, although as much for passenger work as goods, and while the LSWR began to build 4-6-0s for freight traffic in the early years of the 20th century, they too were just as much at home on passenger trains. None ever totally ousted the various classes of 0-6-0 as long as steam lasted in Dorset.

In 1850 Joseph Beattie took over from Gooch and his reign of 21 years resulted in a look which came to characterise the mid-Victorian LSWR. Three of his 2-4-0Ts lasted into British Railways days, down in Cornwall, and two of these have been preserved. There is a photograph of one of these working what purports to be the first train to Swanage, although it probably isn't. But there is no doubt the Beattie tank engines were a familiar sight in Dorset, as were his express locomotives. Most of the latter had gone by the end of the century.

Joseph Beattie was succeeded by his son, William

Broadstone Junction box, 25 July 1939. *G. W. Puntis* ▶

George, in 1871. His reign was a brief, sad one. He pinned his faith in a class of large, outside-cylinder 4-4-0s, 20 of them being ordered from Sharp Stewart in Glasgow for delivery in 1876/7. A bogie engine was a pretty revolutionary concept in the 1870s. They might have been just the thing but their piston valves were troublesome and they steamed badly, the directors lost confidence both in them and their designer and poor William George Beattie had to go, jumping before he was pushed. The official reason given for his resignation in 1877 was ill health – 100 years later it would have been called stress. Whatever his state of mind at this sad failure, he came to terms with it and lived on for another 41 years.

Next came William Adams. An engineer of considerable experience, some of it in marine matters, he set about providing the LSWR with a range of locomotives which would see it well into the 20th century. Indeed one of his 'X6' 4-4-0s, No 659 dating from 1895 and originally employed on the heaviest main line expresses, still found work from Dorchester on the daily pick-up goods to Bournemouth in the 1930s – its companion, No 657, was the star of the wonderful Will Hay comedy *Oh, Mr Porter* – while Dorchester shed was home to no less than five of his '02' 0-4-4Ts in 1950. Most remarkably, three of his 4-4-2Ts, originally designed for conveying office workers from the leafy suburbs of Surrey in and out of Waterloo, were still at work on the Lyme Regis branch in the 1960s.

In 1895 Dugald Drummond succeeded Adams and took the company into the 20th century: but for the moment we will leave locomotive matters and return to the development of railways in the county up to that time.

As we have seen, the London & South Western Railway reached Dorchester in 1847. The Great Western had promoted the Wilts, Somerset & Weymouth Railway in June 1845. It would leave the Paddington to Bristol main line at Thingley Junction, west of Chippenham, connect with the Berks & Hants (the Reading-Taunton direct route, destined eventually to become the West of England main line) at Westbury, and continue through Yeovil to Dorchester. However times were bad; the woollen trade, so

vital to the area, was in decline, the population was decreasing, and it was not until 1 September 1856 that Yeovil was reached. Suddenly enthusiasm took a hold and by 20 January 1857 Weymouth was reached. The line was mixed gauge, for the GWR was still a broad gauge railway. Indeed the GWR stipulated that as it had been decent enough to provide narrow gauge tracks for the LSWR to run on between Dorchester and Weymouth, the LSWR should provide broad gauge tracks of an equivalent distance, eight miles, eastwards from Dorchester. These ended in the middle of Winfrith Heath, one of many stretches (there's a lot less now) of uninhabited heathland. One cannot imagine a more useless piece of railway line and, not surprisingly, there is no record of it ever having been used.

The line between Dorchester and Weymouth demanded heavy engineering, a long climb out of the county town beside prehistoric Maiden Castle to the summit in the 814-yard Bincombe Tunnel, at the end of which was a wonderful view across the harbour, the Isle of Portland and the English Channel, and then a steep sweep down into Weymouth. The town now possessed two routes to London, 147.5 miles by the LSWR to Waterloo, 168.5 by the GWR to Paddington. The first GWR train left Weymouth at 6.15am on 20 January 1857 for Yeovil, the first LSWR at 11.55am for Southampton. Weymouth had waited so long for its railway that it decided to wait one more week, to convince itself that the whole thing was not an illusion, before organising the usual inauguration festivities.

Dorchester had, and still has, two stations. The LSWR one had opened 10 years before the GWR reached the town. The latter, coming in from the north by way of Poundbury, a prehistoric settlement (smaller than Maiden Castle but still impressive), would have had to make a wide detour across the water meadows of the River Frome to reach it. In any case the LSWR station, Dorchester South, was most inconveniently arranged. Because it had been planned as part of a through route to Exeter, the station was laid out on an east-west axis. The thwarting of this scheme and the extension to Weymouth meant that

In the normal course of events the 'Bournemouth Belle' did not reach Dorset but on 3 April 1960 it was diverted by the old main line through Ringwood and Broadstone, hence its appearance on Poole Bank behind 'West Country' No 34006 *Bude*. Poole Park lake is to the right. The sea no longer comes right up to the tracks on the left, the land having been reclaimed. *R. A. Panting*

▲ the line had to swing abruptly to the south, leaving a dead end stub to serve the station, in order to avoid a Roman amphitheatre and to connect with the GWR line at Dorchester Junction. Thus trains bound for Weymouth had to run into the station and then reverse out to proceed on their way around the curve, while trains from Weymouth had to perform the same manoeuvre in reverse. Logic should have dictated building platforms on the curves. This was done for down trains in May 1879 but it took another 88 years before the idea penetrated sufficiently deeply for it to have any effect on trains heading in the other direction.

We left Poole in December 1872, with a new station in the heart of the town at the end of the High Street, on the

Poole & Bournemouth Railway. The centre of Poole is quite flat, at sea level, and is virtually surrounded by water. Although convenient, the station was situated on a curve with a level crossing at either end. Both crossings were heavily used by road traffic and there was congestion right from the start. There were also justifiable fears over what might happen if a train approached them at too high a speed and could not stop in time, and therefore Poole Corporation insisted that all trains should stop in Poole station. This has remained the situation virtually down to the present time, at least as far as passenger trains are concerned, although there is now only one level crossing, for pedestrians. The only time I have ever passed through Poole station without stopping was on the record-breaking nonstop run to celebrate electrification through to Weymouth, when on 11 April 1988 two Class 442 Wessex Electrics did the journey from Waterloo in 1hr, 59min, 24sec.

The line from Poole eastwards was not an easy one to build. First Poole Harbour had to be crossed, by means of an embankment. This created a lake on the landward side surrounded by a park, which became one of the town's chief attractions. From there the line climbed steeply, some sections being 1 in 60, through Parkstone and Branksome stations, before levelling out and crossing the county boundary into Hampshire just before reaching the terminus at Bournemouth West. The promoters had hoped to penetrate much further into the town centre, to the

Square, but a number of prominent Bournemouth citizens were resolutely opposed to letting dirty, smoking steam engines sully their beautiful, as they thought, town so the not very distinguished Town Hall eventually occupied the intended site of the Central station. The line opened on 20 July 1874.

At first there were no through trains to or from Waterloo or even Southampton, only Somerset & Dorset ones, nine inwards, eight outwards. Intending London passengers had to change at Wimborne. The crucial link between Bournemouth West and East stations was completed on 28 September 1886. Even then trains from London had still to use the old roundabout route, 'Castleman's Corkscrew', from Brockenhurst to Ringwood, then down through Hurn

◄ 'T9' No 30706 on the old main line near West Moors, with a Bournemouth West to Salisbury train, c1960. *Dr Ian C. Allen*

The now preserved 'T9' No 30120 with the 10.30am Salisbury-Bournemouth West, climbing out of Poole, 2 August 1958. The photographer records that, although running nearly an hour late, the '59-year-old loco made the ascent of Parkstone Bank with eight coaches unaided, including a stop at Parkstone, with apparent ease.' *J. C. Haydon*

to Christchurch. It was not until 5 March 1888 that the present direct main line from Brockenhurst through Hinton Admiral to Christchurch finally came into existence. From then on most trains between London, Southampton and Dorset travelled this route, calling at Bournemouth Central, as East station became in 1893. Some called at Bournemouth West and reversed out, others bypassed it. In order to create the triangle of lines at Branksome, two high viaducts spanning the Bourne Valley had to be built. Constructed of yellow brick, they remain among the most distinctive and elegant structures in the

Christchurch, Bournemouth and Poole conurbation.

It has to be realised what an insignificant place Bournemouth was at the beginning of the railway era. Its first residence dated only from the Napoleonic era. The Dorset Rangers were set up under one Capt Tregonwell to patrol the coast between Poole and Christchurch harbours and watch for possible invaders. In 1810 the captain built himself a house on the banks of the River (a grand word for a stream any self-respecting Ranger could jump over) Bourne near where it entered the sea between pine-covered cliffs. Mrs and all the little Tregonwells joined him.

Once the threat from across the water was over after 1815 they found the mild, healthy climate and the sea air much to their liking. Friends were invited to stay, one of them being Lord Exeter. Eventually, after the deaths of Capt and Mrs Tregonwell, their house was enlarged and became the Royal Exeter Hotel, which it remains to this day.

Meanwhile, Bournemouth's very first hotel, the Bath, had been opened on the other side of the valley. But progress was slow, and throughout the 1840s, 50s and 60s visitors had to hire a horse-driven conveyance to get them to the town from the nearest railhead at either Poole, Ringwood or Christchurch. Eventually, in 1870, when Bournemouth's population had grown to 5,700, the town's first station was opened at the end of a three-and-a-bit-mile-long branch from Christchurch. Unlike many seaside towns, the civic pride of which demanded an edifice of some dignity, the original Bournemouth station was a mean affair.

The trouble was that Bournemouth could not decide whether it really wanted a railway. Always keen to maintain its dignity and air of exclusivity, many of its citizens shivered with horror at what they perceived the arrival of the railway had done to Brighton and Blackpool and determined that if it could not be kept out altogether then it should be kept as far away from the town centre as possible. Others, notably Merton Russell Coates, who had taken over the Bath Hotel and was in the process of turning it into one of the grandest in the country, held the opposite view. He felt that Bournemouth could do with livening up and that a handsome station in the town centre, within sight, by sheer chance, of his hotel, was just what was needed.

Russell Coates became Mayor of Bournemouth. He and his wife Annie were great travellers and entrepreneurs in the finest Victorian traditions, buying up works of art and artefacts from all over the world, which they displayed in a splendid house built in the grounds of the Royal Bath Hotel and which they gave to the town just after World War 1. It is now the very fine Russell Coates Museum and Art Gallery and the family name is rightly revered in the town. However, in his lifetime Merton upset a good few

Bournemouth folk and it is said that some of his foreign expeditions were diplomatic withdrawals in order to let tempers cool on both sides. Although Bournemouth got a much grander station in 1885 designed by William Jacomb, next door to the original one, and a second one at the other end of the town, Bournemouth West, in 1874, the town centre one so desired by Russell Coates and other forward-thinking citizens never did materialise. Nevertheless, the impact the arrival of the railway had on the town was dramatic, the population increasing threefold between 1871 and 1881.

Holidaymakers to Bournemouth tended to belong to the middle rather than the working classes and did not object to hiring transport to convey them from the station to their boarding houses or hotels. By 1900 the population was approaching 60,000, this almost entirely due to the excellent services provided by the London & South Western Railway and, to a much lesser extent, the Somerset & Dorset. Bournemouth had become a municipal borough in 1890, it had a pier, a town hall, an orchestra which would become the world-famous Bournemouth Symphony Orchestra, many elegant villas and handsome churches in which John Betjeman would delight 50 years later, and three horse-bus companies. Something vastly more up to date than the latter was in the offing for in 1901 British Electric Traction began operating trams in Poole through a subsidiary known as the Poole Light Railways, and put a bill before Parliament to extend across the Dorset border to Bournemouth. This stung Bournemouth Corporation into action and 1902 it was operating its own electric tramcars, one of the first routes linking the Central station with the town centre. Far from Poole invading Bournemouth the opposite happened and in 1905 the Hampshire authority took out a 30-year lease to run the Poole network. The depot and works were built alongside the railway line complete with a siding for coal to be delivered to the generating station.

With the expiry of the lease Hants & Dorset motorbuses replaced trams in Poole in 1935, while between 1934 and 1936 a fleet of trolleybuses replaced Bournemouth's trams. Ten of the more modern were bought for further service in

Llandudno and lasted there until 1956, only 13 years before trolleybuses disappeared from the streets of Bournemouth. As a consequence of their survival on the north Wales coast into the preservation era, one tram, Bournemouth No 85, a UEC-bodied open-topped car on Brill bogies dating from the 1920s, came back to its home town where it has been restored to its original yellow and chocolate livery and is in working order – although it does not actually have anywhere to operate.

The success of the trams put an end to any possible extension of the railway network in Bournemouth and Poole. The considerable distance of both West and Central stations from the commercial centre of Bournemouth discouraged commuter traffic, with which the trams were much better placed to cope. Although Poole, Parkstone and Branksome stations handled a certain amount, the absence of any railway link to the growing northern suburbs has ensured that the amount of suburban business handled by the railways in Bournemouth and Poole has never been very significant.

A picture which clearly illustrates the steep gradient through Buckhorn Weston Tunnel near Gillingham on the West of England main line. 'Battle of Britain' No 34065 *Hurricane* has charge of an 11-coach Waterloo-bound express *c*1952.
W. Vaughan Jenkins

THE BRANCH LINES

We have noted the existence of various branch lines, now let us take a closer look at them individually. The West of England main line through Gillingham to Sherborne opened on 7 May 1860, the section on to Yeovil opened on 1 June that year and by 19 July 1860 trains were running through to Exeter. However the only branch off the route which is of concern to us, that from the carpet-making town of Axminster to Lyme Regis, was of much later date. Although there had long been proposals, the inhabitants of the one-time port, now a resort inextricably linked with Jane Austen, had to wait until the present century before the railway reached them. The branch, with one

intermediate station at Combpyne, opened on 24 August 1903. The LSWR worked it from the start and provided through carriages from Waterloo, which in Southern Railway days took a little over four hours. Lyme Regis station was built on a cliff above the hilly little town, a site which would help seal its fate 60 years later.

Bridport, a town of some substance and famous for its rope-making works, was linked to the GWR Yeovil to Weymouth line at Maiden Newton on 12 November 1857, the branch being worked by that company. The two intermediate stations were Toller, in the delightfully named

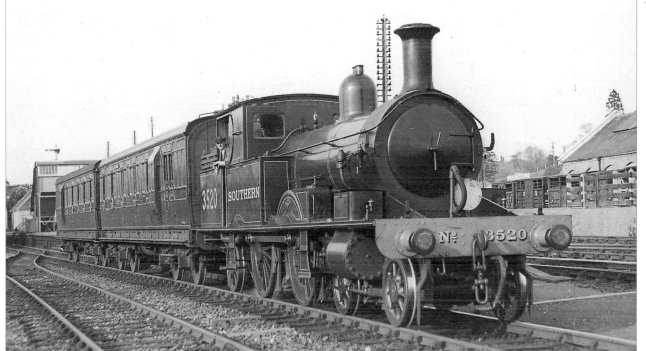

The Lyme Regis branch was chiefly famous for the ancient Adams '0415' class 4-4-2Ts which worked it for so many years. The first of them (there were 71 in all) entered service in 1882 and they virtually monopolised London suburban services in their early years. They were only rendered obsolete when electrification began in 1915. They then gravitated out into the country and, on being replaced by more modern Drummond engines on these less demanding duties, were broken up. Two found a home at Lyme Regis (Exmouth Junction actually, but the Lyme Regis branch was their workplace). By now on the duplicate list, they stayed there as no other engines could cope with the gradients and curves. By the end of the 1920s they had been returned to capital stock and No 3520 is seen in May 1934 with its train of two former LSWR brake composites at Axminster, where the branch connected with the West of England main line.
Ian Allan Library

village of Toller Porcorum, and Powerstock. An extension to Bridport harbour, renamed West Bay, opened on 31 March 1884.

Further down the main line, Upwey became the junction for the Abbotsbury branch on 9 November 1885 (and was appropriately renamed Upwey Junction). There were three intermediate stations: Upwey, Coryates Halt and Portesham. It was always worked by the GWR, being absorbed in 1896.

The Portland branch, leaving the main line just outside Weymouth station, opened on 16 October 1865. It was mixed gauge, although the broad gauge tracks were probably never used, and worked jointly by the GWR and the LSWR. The broad gauge disappeared from GWR lines in Dorset by 1874. There were other lines on the Isle of Portland, the Easton & Church Hope and the Breakwater Railways, for stone and Admiralty traffic, the goods and passenger network being complete and worked by the two main line companies by 1 September 1902. In 1909 Melcombe Regis station, alongside the main Weymouth one and just before the viaduct which carried the branch over the harbour, was opened.

Much the latest of all the Dorset branches – or was it a long siding? – was that to the nuclear power station on Winfrith Heath between Wool and Moreton, which opened in the 1960s.

The Swanage branch opened on 20 May 1885. Worked from the beginning by the LSWR, the promoters hoped to take the direct route from Wareham station through the town but were forced westwards to a junction at Worgret.

The one intermediate station was at Corfe Castle. As at Lyme Regis and West Bay, the arrival of the railway virtually killed off its terminus as a commercial port, turning it instead into a resort. Swanage was not only provided with through carriages from Waterloo but at the height of the summer season complete trains were put on for holidaymakers, some arriving from the Midlands and the North of England by way of the Somerset & Dorset. In the 1930s the 11.22am restaurant car train from Waterloo arrived at Swanage 3hr 18min later.

The opening of the railway to Weymouth encouraged both the LSWR and GWR to promote shipping services between the Dorset port and the Channel Islands. The LSWR one did not last long and the company decided to concentrate on its traditional Southampton service but the GWR-backed one continued and by 1887 was being provided by new GWR-owned boats. A series of improvements was carried out at Weymouth Quay; a new pier was built, the tramway extended so that passengers could walk straight from ship to train, and by 1889, when 7,776 passengers were carried during the summer season, the overall time between Paddington and Guernsey was reduced to less than 12 hours. The best time, weather permitting, between Paddington and Jersey in 1892 was 10.5 hours. For seven years between 1878 and 1885 there was even a service between Weymouth and Cherbourg. The overall time from Paddington to Paris was 21 hours. Although not a success this was not the last attempt by any means to establish French cross-Channel services at Weymouth.

Thus the pattern of railway lines in Dorset was established. It would not stay intact for very long, with the first motor cars making their dusty way into Dorset's rural fastness just as the rail network was reaching completion. As in so much of Britain it would be the Beeching era of the 1960s which would see its retrenchment.

◄ Eventually it was found that the London Midland Region Class 2 2-6-2Ts, which had been extensively used on the Southern Region, could work the Lyme Regis branch and the 4-4-2Ts were withdrawn. No 488, the ex-EKR engine, was bought by the Bluebell Railway, where it remains to this day. 2-6-2T No 41291 is seen in charge of a single GWR-design auto-coach, which replaced Southern Railway carriages at the end of the branch's existence, near Combpyne with the 12.40 from Lyme Regis to Axminster, 10 March 1965, eight months before the branch closed.
W. L. Underhay

West Bay, August 1947. Although this section had closed for regular passenger traffic in 1930, the occasional excursion still ran and, as can be seen, it was still open for goods.
G. W. Puntis

The Bridport branch (West Bay was an extension from Bridport itself) lasted beyond the steam age until 1975. It connected with the Dorchester-Yeovil line at Maiden Newton. Regular motive power in later years were '45xx' and '4575' 2-6-2Ts. Here Churchward No 4507 has charge of the usual two-coach Collett B Set parked under the branch platform's diminutive overall roof at Maiden Newton and waits for passengers off the Yeovil-bound stopping train hauled by No 5978 *Bodinnick Hall*, a Weymouth resident, its train consisting of Collett corridor carriages; 22 March 1958. *C. P. Boocock*

◄ Closure notice of the Abbotsbury branch, which took effect from 1 December 1952. *R. C. Riley*

◄◄ Dean 0-4-2T No 1427 leaves Coryates Halt with an auto-train for Abbotsbury, January 1936. *Dr Ian C. Allen*

◄ In this picture Dean 0-4-2T No 531 has charge of a Dean bogie full brake as well as a Churchward auto-coach as it enters Abbotsbury station in September 1929. It is running on flat-bottomed rail, manufactured by Krupps, which had been there ever since the branch was opened in 1884. *Dr Ian C. Allen*

Ivatt 2-6-2T No 41284 on the high embankment above Weymouth Town football ground, with the last train on the Portland branch, 27 March 1965. *Tony Trood*

'B4' 0-4-0T No 30093, one of the dock tanks introduced by Adams in 1891, performs a task it was designed for on Poole Quay, 25 August 1954. Tied up alongside is the coaster SS *John Evelyn* of Leith, almost as old as the 'B4'. *R. C. Riley*

Hamworthy Goods, the original Poole station, long confined to goods traffic, almost deserted save for a gentleman minding the platform edge and a Morris Minor tourer, 27 August 1954. *R. C. Riley*

EARLY 20TH CENTURY

The first reaction to road competition took the form of self-propelled steam railmotors. Both the LSWR and the GWR introduced them in Dorset, the former around Bournemouth, the latter in the Weymouth and Dorchester areas. The GWR was a more enthusiastic and thorough user of the steam railmotor than any other British main line company and opened a number of halts; Monkton & Came Golf Links (one assumes the halt was big enough to accommodate its nameboard!), Bincombe, and Upwey Wishing Well for example. The steam railmotor was dirty and rather uncomfortable and it would have to await the perfection of the diesel engine for the notion of a self-propelled non electric railway carriage to become truly viable, but the GWR vehicles came the nearest to achieving success, the last not disappearing until the 1930s. Many were converted to push-pull trailers and one such, which has been preserved by the Great Western Society, is to be reconverted back to its original steam-propelled condition.

World War 1 made great demands on the railways of Dorset. Military camps were set up all over the county, at Bovington, Lulworth, Blandford and Wareham for example, and Portland was one of the country's premier

Dean 0-4-2T No 542 takes water at Evershot in September 1929 while working a stopping train from Yeovil Pen Mill to Weymouth. The coach on the right is a Churchward auto-trailer, that on the left a Dean clerestory, presumably attached behind No 542 to provide extra accommodation.
Dr Ian C. Allen

naval bases. Poole and Weymouth saw much traffic to and from France and the insatiable demands of the Western Front.

The Grouping did not immediately bring about any great changes, except that Southern olive green replaced the LSWR shade on locomotives and salmon and pink on carriages. The Great Western Railway went on its merry way as though nothing had changed and in 1935 became the only British main line company ever to celebrate its centenary. The recession following the Wall Street Crash of 1929 ensured that less was made of this historic event than might otherwise have been the case. The main 'Cornish Riviera' train was given two superb new sets of carriages, the Centenary Stock, but although a slip carriage off this train reached Weymouth each afternoon at 1.52, having left Paddington at 10.30am, it was of an older, standard design. The GWR and the Southern Railway were still competing for the Dorchester and Weymouth trade; a restaurant car train left Waterloo five minutes after the

'Cornish Riviera' left Paddington, and its Weymouth carriages arrived at their destination at 1.56pm, four minutes after the through GWR slip carriage.

Dugald Drummond had provided the LSWR with a highly efficient fleet of 4-4-0s and 0-4-4Ts. His 4-6-0s were far less successful but his successor, Robert Urie, had remedied this with the 'S15' and 'H15' mixed-traffic 4-6-0s and the 'N15' express engines. All these classes served the Southern Railway well. R. E. L. Maunsell, the first Southern Railway CME, built further examples of all three, the modified 'N15s' becoming the famous 'King Arthur' class. The 'N15s' had a long career working Bournemouth and Weymouth expresses, although Drummond's final 4-4-0s, the 'D15s', took some replacing on the Bournemouth expresses for they were handsome, powerful, fast machines. I bought a delightful reprint of an Edwardian 'Father Tuck's Express Train Panorama with Movable Pictures' in, of all places, the Seaport Museum on the Hudson River, New York in 1997 which featured in the

Wolverhampton-built 0-4-2T No 215, a design introduced in 1876, at Weymouth c1930.
J. L. Smith collection

▶

No 302, one of the long-lived Drummond 'T9' 4-4-0s, shunts a Maunsell corridor at Weymouth, April 1939. *K. O'B. Nichols*

most accurate detail a 'D15' about to set off from Waterloo for Bournemouth and Weymouth with an 'M7' in the background.

The Dean/Churchward 4-4-0s of the GWR were as numerous as Drummond's 4-4-0s in the Weymouth area, but they too began to be replaced by 4-6-0s in the 1920s, first by Churchward's 'Saints', then by Collett's mixed-traffic 'Halls' and 'Granges'. In 1926 Maunsell introduced what was claimed to be Britain's most powerful express engine, No 850 *Lord Nelson*. Fifteen more were built a little later. Beautifully proportioned, the 'Nelsons' soon appeared on the Weymouth line. On occasions they could outperform all other Southern Railway classes but they had to be handled with care, and it was not until Bulleid took over from Maunsell in 1937 and carried out various modifications to their cylinders and fitted them with Lemaitre blast pipes that they came into their own. From

then on they were concentrated on the Bournemouth and Weymouth line until withdrawal in the 1960s.

Although nominally not as powerful as the 'Lord Nelsons', Collett's 'Castle' class of 1923 was just about the most successful passenger 4 6 0 ever seen in Britain. The class continued to be built until 1950; examples were shedded at Westbury and Weymouth for the principal Paddington expresses.

The 2-6-0 was as versatile a type as one could wish for. The first really modern ones, the GWR '43xxs', were introduced in 1911 and Maunsell soon followed with the 'N' class of 1917 and the larger wheeled 'Us' of 1928. All of these performed every sort of duty in Dorset from express passenger to pick-up goods until virtually the end of steam. It gave enthusiasts great pleasure to see the preserved Collett 2-6-0 No 7325 revisiting the Weymouth to Yeovil line in November 1997.

Southern Railway 'Schools' class 4-4-0 No 929 *Malvern*, newly repainted in malachite green, rolls a three-coach train through Radipole Halt on the approach to Weymouth. *Malvern* was one of the six engines of this class repainted in this livery in 1938 for working the 'Bournemouth Limited'. The pagoda-type shelters, much favoured by the GWR for its halts, lasted into the 1970s. *J. L. Smith collection*

▲ The GWR introduced the first complete corridor train in the United Kingdom and the LSWR was also forward looking in carriage design, so that by Grouping the bogie carriage was the norm on both companies' lines, although it would be several decades before the non-corridor coach disappeared. In the summer of 1929 the Southern Railway introduced a named train, the 'Bournemouth Limited', made up of the latest carriages. There were through portions for Weymouth and Swanage. In 1938 what were claimed to be brand new carriages were provided – they were not quite new but they were repainted in the latest, bright, malachite green livery and given refurbished interiors. Gone was the varnished wood, replaced by Rexine. It looked handsomely up-to-date. The two-coach Swanage section left at 7.44am, joined the three-coach Weymouth section at Wareham, leaving there at 8.14, joined the six coaches, including a dining car, from Bournemouth West at Bournemouth Central, left there at 8.40 and ran nonstop to Waterloo, arriving at 10.38. Two hours later it set off back to Hampshire and Dorset. Motive power was a 'Schools' 4-4-0. These, the last and best of all the many designs of 4-4-0, had been introduced by

Maunsell for the restricted-clearance Hastings line in 1930 but had proved to be so outstanding that the class was expanded to 40 members and used on expresses all over the Southern Railway. Ten were transferred to Bournemouth shed in 1937, six being repainted in the new malachite green, in which they looked superb, and in 1938 No 928 *Stowe* reached what was then the highest speed ever recorded on Southern lines, when it came galloping along the straight, level stretch through Wool at 95mph. *Stowe* is still at work, preserved on the Bluebell Railway.

Bulleid's appointment as CME of the Southern Railway heralded the eventual appearance of what would be the most revolutionary steam engines ever to work in Dorset, a design which would come to dominate the final decade of steam and establish almost a monopoly of the last steam main line in Britain.

Rather remarkably the largest goods engines to find regular employment in Dorset before Nationalisation belonged neither to the GWR nor the Southern but to the Somerset & Dorset. These were 11 2-8-0s, designed at Derby and introduced in 1914. They were pure Midland in every respect, although nothing as big worked on the Midland Railway itself. They were used chiefly on the most heavily graded section of the Somerset & Dorset north of Evercreech but they often came down to Poole and Bournemouth. On summer weekends they were regularly employed as passenger engines, even taking charge of the line's most celebrated train, the 'Pines Express'. This began running in 1910 as a regular, all-year-round, restaurant car express between Manchester and Bournemouth, although it was not named at first. By the 1930s such was its fame that you could buy a Hornby 'O' gauge 'Pines Express' train set. Despite proving very successful, the '7F' 2-8-0s were never added to and they spent their long lives working among the hills of Somerset and Dorset.

The S&D retained its independence at the Grouping but in 1933 its parlous financial state saw its joint owners take it over completely. To most casual observers it seemed the LMS was now in charge, for its locomotives and carriages assumed LMS livery. In fact responsibility was shared, the Southern taking over signalling and track maintenance.

Inevitably the ubiquitous Stanier '5MT' 4-6-0s appeared and displaced older designs, although the Midland type 4-4-0s, 0-6-0s and 0-4-4Ts remained for some years. After World War 2, for the first time ever, locomotives of Southern design took up regular work in the shape of Bulleid Light Pacifics. Later BR Standard designs appeared, most notably the '9F' 2-10-0s. These included No 92220 *Evening Star*, British Railways' very last steam engine, which was built at Swindon in 1960. It was withdrawn a mere five years later but has reappeared on various parts of the network in preservation days.

World War 2 made demands on the railways of Dorset as great as the 1914-18 war had done, particularly in the period leading up to D-Day and afterwards. As a small boy living at Bournemouth in 1944-5, the world to me seemed full of American soldiers bound for the front. Trains were packed and I can remember what seemed like endless journeys either standing in corridors or, once, in a dimly lit guard's van smelling strongly of stale fish. Despite restrictions on material of just about every sort there was still a need for new locomotives. These were supposed to be of mixed traffic or freight design but Bulleid, who had

◄ Unusual motive power for an auto-coach: Churchward 2-6-0 No 8329 on Upwey Bank, 27 August 1938.
J. L. Smith collection

The unusual sight of a
Pullman express
approaching Dorchester
South on its way to
Weymouth, 16 September
1931. It had left Waterloo at
10.30am. The engine is
'Lord Nelson' 4-6-0 No 862
Lord Collingwood. One
wonders just what this
working was, of only four
carriages, scarcely a
demanding load for the
company's premier express
engine; possibly it was in
connection with some
special naval event at
Portland. *G. Puntis*

One of Adams's elderly 'X6'
4-4-0s, No 659, dating from
1895, heads an up goods
across the River Frome
water meadows east of
Wool, *c*1930. Originally
employed on the heaviest
expresses, the 'X6s',
William Adams's last
passenger design,
gravitated to less
demanding work in
Southern Railway days.
No 659 was at this time
shedded at Dorchester and
this was its regular duty.
Sister engine No 657 was
the star of the celebrated
Will Hay film *Oh, Mr Porter*.
No 659 was condemned in
1943. *L&GRP*

come to the Southern after years of working on the LNER with Sir Nigel Gresley, the most gifted and original designer of his era, was determined to put his own highly individual ideas into practice, and somehow managed to persuade the authorities that *Channel Packet*, an out and out express passenger design if ever there was one, nevertheless qualified. This extraordinary looking, 'air-smoothed' – streamlined is what anyone else would have called it – 4-6-2 was completed at Eastleigh in March 1941. Nine further Pacifics of the 'Merchant Navy' class appeared in 1941-2, followed by 10 more in 1944-5. They were allegedly chiefly intended for Kent Coast boat trains, which makes their construction during the war years even more remarkable, but they actually worked almost exclusively on

the Western Section and appeared regularly west of Bournemouth. A final 10 came out under British Railways in 1948-9, by which time production of their smaller brothers, the 'West Country' and 'Battle of Britain' Pacifics was in full swing

The first of these, No 21C101 *Exeter*, was completed in 1945 and by January 1951, when production ended, 110 had been built. Their names were divided between squadrons, aerodromes, etc associated with the Battle of Britain and places in the West Country. Dorset featured on a number of the 'West Countries' although this did not mean that you could assume that the engine would ever be able to reach its home town – for instance the nearest No 21C135 ever got to Shaftesbury was when it passed along the West of England main line through Semley, several miles to the north. British Railways got rid of Bulleid's peculiar numbering system, the 'Merchant Navies' being renumbered in the 35xxx series, the Light Pacifics in the 34xxx.

Excellent though both classes were in some respects, they were troublesome and expensive to maintain and within four years of the newest taking to the rails, authority was given for their extensive rebuilding. All the 'Merchant Navies' were done and around half of the Light Pacifics before it became clear that steam would not last much longer and the project came to an end. Thus some of the unrebuilt Light Pacifics survived into the preservation era along with their rebuilt brothers.

Southern Railway timetable, 1947. ▶

A railtour to the Lyme Regis branch in June 1953 produced this most unusual combination of the regular Adams 4-4-2T No 30583 and a visiting Stroudley 'Terrier' 'A1X' No 32662, seen here pulling out of Lyme Regis. The leading carriage is an LSWR eight-compartment non-corridor brake third. ▶▶

J. B. McCann/Colour-Rail

SOUTHERN–Western Section 336

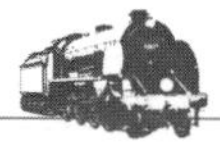

CHRISTCHURCH, BOURNEMOUTH, POOLE, and WIMBORNE

Week Days

Miles		mrn	mrn	mrn	mrn	mrn	mrn	mrn	mrn	mrn	mrn	mrn
—	Christchurch...dep.	2 3	5 30	..	..	..	6 5	6 30	From Dorchester (dep 7 0 mrn) p. 330	..	7 29	..
1¾	Pokesdown ●........	..	5 33	..	..	..	—	6 37		..	7 37	..
2½	Boscombe...........	..	5 36	..	..	..	—	6 43		..	7 41	..
3½	Bournemouth Central arr.	2 12	5 42	..	..	..	6 15	6 48		..	7 45	..
	Bournemouth Central dep	2 24	5 47	6 25	..	..	6 32	7 6		7 42	7 50	..
7	Bournemouth West.	..	..	..	6 48	..	6 42	..		..	8 0	8 10
8¼	Branksome........	..	5 53	6 32	..	..	3	7 13		7 48	..	8 14
9¼	Parkstone L........	..	5 57	6 37	..	..		7 20		7 53	..	8 18
11¼	Poole..............	2 37	6 3	6 44	6 59	..	—	7 30		7 57	..	8 23
13¼	Creekmoor Halt.....	..	..	6 49	..	..	..	..		8 1	..	8 30
14¼	Broadstone Z........	..	..	6 53	7 9	7 14	—	..	7 45	8 6	..	8 34
17¼	Wimborne 339...arr.	..	..	6 59	..	7 19	..	..	7 51	8 12	..	8 40

	mrn	mrn	mrn	mrn	mrn	mrn	mrn	mrn	mrn	mrn	mrn	mrn	mrn
Christchurch...dep.	..	8 21	..	8 39	9 11	..	..	..	9 59	..	..	..	1142
Pokesdown ●........	..	8 27	..	8 45	9 17	..	..	..	10 5	..	..	..	1148
Boscombe...........	..	8 29	..	8 49	9 20	..	..	..	10 8	..	..	..	1152
Bournemouth Central arr.	..	8 33	..	8 53	9 24	..	..	..	1012	..	..	..	1156
Bournemouth Central dep	..	8 38	..	8 57	9 29	..	..	..	1018	1119	..	1124	..
Bournemouth West.	8 45	8 43	8 50	..	..	9 45	10 0	..	..	..	1140	1134	..
Branksome........	8 48	..	8 54	9 5	9 37	..	10 4	..	1026	..	..	..	..
Parkstone L........	8 51	..	8 58	9 9	9 41	..	10 8	..	1030	..	..	..	..
Poole..............	8 56	..	9 4	9 16	9 48	9 54	1014	1032	1038	1133	1149	..	..
Creekmoor Halt.....	..	..	9 9	..	..	..	1019	1036	—	..	..	..	..
Broadstone Z........	..	..	9 15	..	..	..	1024	1042	..	..	1158	..	..
Wimborne 339...arr.	..	..	..	..	..	..	1031	1048	..	..	..	..	..

Week Days—continued

	mrn	aft	aft	aft	aft	aft	aft	aft	aft	aft	aft	aft SX	aft SO	aft SO	aft SO	aft
Christchurch...dep.	1158	..	1218	..	..	..	..	..	1 15	..	2 7	..	—	..	—	..
Pokesdown ●........	12 2	..	1223	..	..	..	..	..	1 21	..	2 14	..	—	..	—	..
Boscombe...........	12 5	..	..	..	..	..	..	..	1 24	..	2 18	..	—	..	—	..
Bournemouth Central arr.	12 9	..	1230	..	..	..	..	..	1 28	..	2 22	..	—	..	..	..
Bournemouth Central dep	1212	..	1233	..	..	1253	1 1	..	..	..	2 24	2 57	3 0	3 12	3 4	..
Bournemouth West	1222	1237	1243	1247	1255	1 3	..	1 18	..	2 35	2 34	..	—	..	3 14	3 30
Branksome........	..	1240	..	..	1259	..	1 7	1 22	..	2 38	..	3 3	..	3 18	..	..
Parkstone L........	..	1244	..	..	1 4	..	1 11	1 26	..	2 41	—	3 7	..	3 22	..	3 37
Poole..............	..	1249	..	1 1	1 11	—	1 18	1 33	..	2 45	—	3 13	3 13	3 27	—	3 43
Creekmoor Halt.....	..	1253	..	..	1 16	—	..	1 39	..	2 52	..	..	..	..	..	..
Broadstone Z........	..	1257	..	..	1 27	..	..	1 46	..	2 57	..	..	..	..	..	3 52
Wimborne 339..arr.	..	1 3	..	..	..	..	..	1 53	..	3 4	..	..	..	..	..	..

	aft	aft	aft	aft	aft	aft	aft	aft	aft	aft	aft	aft	aft	aft
Christchurch...dep.	3 21	..	4 5	..	..	..	4 47	..	5 5	..	..	..	6 15	..
Pokesdown ●........	3 27	..	4 11	..	..	..	4 55	..	5 12	..	..	..	6 21	..
Boscombe...........	3 30	..	4 14	..	..	..	4 58	..	5 15	..	..	..	..	..
Bournemouth Central arr.	3 34	..	4 18	..	..	..	5 2	..	5 20	..	..	..	6 28	..
Bournemouth Central dep	3 36	..	4 20	4 28	..	4 50	..	..	5 23	5 48	5 34	..	6 30	..
Bournemouth West	3 46	4 32	4 30	..	4 47	..	..	5 15	5 33	..	6 4	6 40	6 40	6 50
Branksome........	..	4 36	..	..	4 51	4 56	..	5 19	..	5 56	..	..	..	6 54
Parkstone L........	..	4 40	..	..	4 55	5 0	..	5 24	..	6 0	..	6 47	..	6 58
Poole..............	..	4 45	..	4 39	5 1	5 6	..	5 33	..	6 7	..	6 53	..	7 3
Creekmoor Halt.....	..	4 49	..	..	5 6	..	..	5 39	..	..	..	6 58	..	7 7
Broadstone Z........	..	4 53	..	..	5 10	..	..	5 45	..	..	..	7 4	..	7 11
Wimborne 339..arr.	..	4 59	..	..	5 16	..	..	..	..	..	..	..	..	7 17

Week Days—continued

	aft	aft	aft	aft	aft	aft	aft	aft B	aft	aft	aft	aft	aft	aft	aft SO	aft	aft
Christchurch...dep	6 35	..	..	..	..	..	7 27	Dep Hamworthy Junc. 8 17 aft.	..	8 16	..	..	..	9 22	..	..	1039
Pokesdown ●........	6 41	..	..	..	..	..	7 33		..	8 23	..	..	..	9 28	..	..	1045
Boscombe...........	6 44	..	..	..	..	..	7 36		..	8 27	..	..	..	9 31	..	..	1049
Bournemouth Central arr.	6 48	..	..	..	..	..	7 40		..	8 31	..	..	..	9 35	..	..	1053
Bournemouth Central dep.	..	6 50	7 4	7 10	7 20	..	..		..	8 34	8 55	9 1	9 18	9 39	..	..	1056
Bournemouth West	..	7 0	—	7 20	..	7 43	..		8 50	8 44	..	9 11	..	9 49	10 0	1049	11 6
Branksome........	..	..	..	..	7 26	7 47	..		8 53	..	..	..	9 24	..	10 4	1052	..
Parkstone L........	..	..	..	..	7 30	7 50	..		8 57	..	..	..	9 28	..	10 9	1056	..
Poole..............	..	..	[illegible]	..	7 36	7 57	..		9 2	..	9 9	..	9 34	..	1017	11 3	..
Creekmoor Halt.....	..	..	..	..	..	8 3	..		9 6	..	..	..	..	..	..	..	..
Broadstone Z........	..	..	..	..	..	8 7	..	8 25	9 10	..	..	—	..	..	1027	1113	..
Wimborne 339..arr.	..	..	..	..	..	8 13	..	8 41	9 16	..	..	..	..	..	..	1119	..

Sundays

	mrn	mrn	mrn	mrn	mrn	mrn	aft	aft	aft	aft
Christchurch...dep	2 3	6 20	..	9 43	..	1150	1210	..	..	1 21
Pokesdown ●........	..	6 28	..	9 49	..	1154	1216	..	..	1 27
Boscombe...........	..	6 32	..	9 52	..	1159	1219	..	..	1 30
Bournemouth Central arr.	2 12	6 36	..	9 56	..	12 3	1223	..	..	1 34
Bournemouth Central dep.	2 24	3	8 5	..	10 7	..	1225	1 2	1 10	1 36
Bournemouth West	..		..	..	..	..	1234	1 12	..	1 46
Branksome........	..	..	8 13	..	1015	..	..	..	1 18	..
Parkstone L........	..	..	8 18	..	1019	..	..	..	1 22	..
Poole..............	2 37	..	8 25	..	1027	..	..	..	1 29	..
Creekmoor Halt.....	..	—	8 29	..	..	..	..	..	..	..
Broadstone Z........	..	—	8 33	..	..	..	..	..	..	..
Wimborne 339..arr.	..	..	8 40	..	..	..	..	..	..	..

Sundays—continued

	aft	aft	aft	aft	aft	aft	aft	aft	aft	aft	aft
Christchurch...dep.	2 6	..	2 43	..	4 1	..	7 1	9 17	..	..	11 1
Pokesdown ●........	2 13	..	[illegible]	..	4 8	..	7 7	9 23	..	..	11 7
Boscombe...........	2 16	..	[illegible]	..	4 11	..	7 10	9 27	..	..	1110
Bournemouth Central arr.	2 20	..	[illegible]	..	4 15	..	7 14	9 31	..	..	1114
Bournemouth Central dep.	2 22	2 27	..	..	4 17	4 22	..	9 35	9 40	..	..
Bournemouth West.	2 32	..	..	3 21	4 27	..	..	..	9 50	10 7	..
Branksome........	..	2 33	..	3 28	..	4 30	..	9 43	..	1011	..
Parkstone L........	..	2 39	..	3 31	..	4 34	..	9 47	—	1014	..
Poole..............	..	2 46	..	3 36	..	4 39	..	9 53	..	1019	..
Creekmoor Halt.....	..	..	..	3 40	..	..	..	..	..	1023	..
Broadstone Z........	..	..	..	3 45	..	..	..	..	..	1027	..
Wimborne 339..arr.	..	..	..	3 51	..	..	..	..	—	1033	..

3 Third class only
B From Dorchester (dep. 7 32 aft), page 333
L Station for Sandbanks

● For Eastern Bournemouth
S O Saturdays only
S X Saturdays excepted
Z Broadstone (Dorset)

With Lyme Bay in the distance and a heap of coal in the foreground, No 30583 takes a breather at Lyme Regis, 14 July 1960. This engine is now preserved in LSWR livery on the Bluebell Railway. *R. C. Riley*

No 30584 pulls out of Combpyne for Lyme Regis, 9 July 1959. *R. C. Riley*

GWR-built 'Grange' 4-6-0 No 6804 *Brockington Grange* pulls out of Yeovil Pen Mill with a rake of GWR carriages for Weymouth, July 1958.
S. C. Townroe/Colour-Rail

Dorset still sees steam on the main line from time to time. Former LMS Stanier 2-6-0 No 2968 and former GWR Collett No 7325 head out of Yeovil Pen Mill on a damp November day in 1997 to pick up the coaches of the appropriately named 'Hardy Flyer' at Weymouth.
M. H. C. Baker

Forty-one years earlier another GWR 2-6-0, this time Churchward No 5323, waits for the road at Dorchester Junction at the head of a down goods, with the West station in the distance. The Portland stone goods shed is on the right, while insulated containers are in the sidings in the foreground alongside a withdrawn 70ft toplight concertina dating from the early years of the century. *R. C. Riley*

Dorchester West became Southern Region property in BR days, hence the green and yellow paint. The immaculate former LSWR 'M7' 0-4-4T No 30107 and its train of two former LSWR carriages would not have been a normal sight and is calling during a railtour in June 1958. *G. H. Hunt/Colour-Rail*

Quite close to home, 'West Country' Pacific No 34105 *Swanage* is about to depart from Dorchester South with a Waterloo train, 10 July 1956. In the yard is a Southern National coach; the bogic goods brake van is a most interesting vehicle, being one of the conversions from a former LBSCR overhead motorcoach. Such a vehicle seemed to be a regular fixture at this spot and presumably resided there between working up the line towards Bournemouth. *Swanage* is preserved in its original form on the Mid-Hants Railway and has visited its home town in recent years. *R. C. Riley*

◄ Dorchester shed in April 1952. Situated immediately east of the station on the down side, it was reached by a rather awkward connection straight into the shed. On view are Urie 'King Arthur' 4-6-0 No 30743 *Lyonesse*, three Adams '02' 0-4-4Ts and on the far right a Urie 'H15' 4-6-0. *S. C. Townroe/Colour-Rail*

A pair of GWR 4-6-0s,
Nos 6999 *Capel Dewi Hall*
and 6870 *Bodicote Grange*,
south of the disused
platforms of Monkton &
Came Halt with a down
Weymouth express in June
1963. Maiden Castle, the
most extensive prehistoric
settlement in Britain, lies a
few hundred yards away off
the left of the picture.
Tommy Tomalin/Colour-Rail

'T9' 4-4-0 No 30119 in
immaculate malachite green
emerges from Bincombe
Tunnel and drifts down the
bank towards Weymouth,
May 1952. No 30119's
wonderful condition is
explained by the fact that it
was especially kept for
working royal and other
specials. Despite this it was
withdrawn seven months
after this picture was taken.
S. C. Townroe/Colour-Rail

Rebuilt 'Merchant Navy' Pacific No 35030, very clean but nameless, backs out of Weymouth depot on 12 June 1967. *R. C. Riley*

No 35030 eases gently down towards Weymouth yard to take out the 'Channel Islands Boat Express' which will be brought from the quay by an '03' class diesel, on 12 June 1967, one month before the end of steam between Waterloo and Weymouth. *R. C. Riley*

◄ On 8 July 1979 the Great Western Society bought its vintage train of restored Swindon-designed coaches to Weymouth and it is seen here passing the massed ranks of fishing boats on its way to the harbour station. *M. H. Baker*

▲

On 3 July 1966 'Black 5' No 45493 and Rebuilt 'West Country' No 34100 *Appledore* are seen passing Weymouth shed with the return Locomotive Club of Great Britain 'V2 Tour' working to Waterloo. The train had travelled via Yeovil Junction and Yeovil Pen Mill. *Hugh Ballantyne*

Wareham station, April 1963. Maunsell 'N' Mogul No 31804 arrives with the 10.10 Dorchester to Eastleigh goods. *Alan Wild*

After passenger traffic on the Swanage branch had gone over to DEMUs, the daily goods train to the clay works at Furzebrook remained steam-hauled until July 1967. On 14 June 1967 rebuilt 'West Country' No 34013, minus nameplates, approaches Worgret Junction with empty clay wagons. Wooden-bodied open wagons of pre-Nationalisation origin, from all four companies, continued to be used for this traffic until the early 1980s. The main line curves away to the right, the branch to the left. *R. C. Riley*

Secundus, an 0-6-0T dating from 1874, which worked on the clay lines in Purbeck and is preserved in the (currently closed) Birmingham Industrial Museum. It is a curious little engine with enclosed motion, a marine boiler and cowcatchers, the latter not a feature of any of the other clay engines, neither steam nor diesel. *M. H. C. Baker*

A scene on the 1ft 10in clay line at Norden, the interchange with the BR Swanage branch, 19 June 1970. *R. C. Riley*

A Simplex diesel with a couple of loaded clay wagons crossing the bridge over the BR line and the present day location of the park and ride station, Norden, 19 June 1970. *R. C. Riley*

Corfe Castle station – and castle – August 1956. 'West Country' Pacific No 34019 *Bideford* stands well out of the station with a lengthy holiday express from Waterloo, composed of 'Ironclad' corridor stock dating from the early 1920s. An 'N' 2-6-0 stands in the siding and the rear LSWR-built carriage of the Wareham-bound push-pull is at the up platform. *S. C. Townroe*

The second and last of the LCGB special runs on the Swanage branch on 7 May 1967 leaves Corfe Castle for Wareham with No 80011 at the head of the train and Unrebuilt 'West Country' No 34023 *Blackmore Vale* (now preserved) at the rear. *Hugh Ballantyne*

LMS-type Class 2 2-6-2T No 41316 pulls out of Corfe Castle with a pair of Bulleid corridors bound for Swanage, July 1965. The sidings to the goods shed have been removed and ivy is beginning to take over the Purbeck stone shed itself. *R. C. Riley*

Steam still flourishes in the Isle of Purbeck. Restored 'M7' 0-4-4T No 30053, once a regular on the branch in BR days and since brought back from the USA, heads a train for Swanage beneath the Purbeck Hills in June 1997. *M. H. C. Baker*

Rebuilt 'West Country'
No 34004, minus
nameplates, heads a
Swanage-bound special of
blue and grey BR Mk 2
stock between Corfe Castle
and Harmans Cross,
11 June 1967. *R. C. Riley*

Now a busy passing place,
Harmans Cross station did
not exist in pre-preservation
days. BR Standards 2-6-4T
No 80104 and '9F' 2-10-0
No 92203 *Black Prince* arrive
from Norden and Corfe
Castle in September 1997.
Although trains from the
Somerset & Dorset regularly
worked down to Swanage
and '9Fs' worked the S&D,
there is no record of a '9F'
coming down the branch in
BR days. The Standard
tanks were, however,
regulars, replacing the
'M7s' in final BR days.
M. H. C. Baker

▲
BR Standard 2-6-4T No 80146 passing Swanage engine shed with a train from Wareham, 4 June 1966. *R. C. Riley*

2-6-2T No 41316 pulls out of Swanage station past the typical LSWR-design signalbox, July 1965. *R. C. Riley* ▶

Another station which has only come into existence in preservation days is Herston Halt. Double-heading was quite common in Southern and BR days but nothing like this spectacle, at Herston in February 1993, had been seen before. Leading is No 30075, a 'USA' 0-6-0T, more or less identical to a class which worked in Southampton Docks (although this particular one carries a fictitious number, having been bought from Yugoslavia), followed by 'M7' No 30053, 'T9' 4-4-0 No 120, and 'Battle of Britain' No 34072 *257 Squadron*, the latter three being representatives of classes regularly seen on the branch in pre-preservation days.
M. H. C. Baker

Blandford station, 4 July 1961. *R. C. Riley*

On 28 December 1965 BR Standard Class 4 2-6-4T No 80039 departs from Blandford with the 12.30pm Templecombe-Bournemouth service. *Hugh Ballantyne*

Derby-built '4F' 0-6-0 No 44557 heads the 6.35am Evercreech Junction-Poole pick-up goods at Bailey Gate, between Blandford and Broadstone, 4 July 1961. *R. C. Riley*

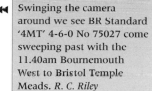

Swinging the camera around we see BR Standard '4MT' 4-6-0 No 75027 come sweeping past with the 11.40am Bournemouth West to Bristol Temple Meads. *R. C. Riley*

BR '9F' 2-10-0 No 92233 heads a neat rake of eight LMS-design corridors near Shepton Montague with the 7.45am Bradford Forster Square-Bournemouth West, 1 September 1962. *R. C. Riley*

The down 'Pines Express', headed by grubby 'West Country' No 34043 *Combe Martin*, entering Sturminster Newton, 1 September 1962. The first carriage is an ex-LNER Gresley corridor third. *R. C. Riley*

The celebrated '9F' 2-10-0 No 92220 *Evening Star*, the last steam locomotive built for BR, which was completed at Swindon in 1960 and is now preserved in the National Collection, crosses the River Stour at Sturminster Newton with a rake of very early Southern Railway-built Bulleid corridors, 1 September 1962. *R. C. Riley*

Sturminster Newton signalbox with a fine display of flowers and vintage motorcycle, 4 July 1961. *R. C. Riley*

STURMINSTER NEWTON

STURMI

67

The first of the very successful but short-lived '9F' 2-10-0s, No 92000, at Corfe Mullen Junction, 4 July 1961. *R. C. Riley*

Maunsell 'Q' 0-6-0 No 30548 with a freight at West Moors, the junction for the Salisbury and Ringwood branches, July 1959. A British Railways Fordson sundries traffic lorry is loading in the yard. *G. H. Hunt/Colour-Rail*

A rather remarkable aerial view of Hamworthy Junction, with BR Standard '4MT' 2-6-0 No 76017 heading for Hamworthy Goods station, the main line to Wareham and Weymouth curving away out of the top of the picture. *Colour-Rail*

The line to Hamworthy Quay was authorised as a branch of the line from Southampton to Dorchester on 21 July 1845 and was opened on 1 June 1847. The station was initially known as Poole, until the opening of the steeply graded line through to Bournemouth from Broadstone via Poole in the early 1870s; thereafter traffic over the now renamed branch declined and passenger services were withdrawn as long ago as `1 July 1896. Evidence of the closed passenger station is clear in this view of the Quay taken on 27 June 1962. A diesel shunter, No D2275, is also visible shunting wagons. The freight-only line survives today. *R. C. Riley*

Peckett 0-4-0ST *Western Pride* in Poole Docks, opposite the Quay, 4 July 1961. *R. C. Riley*

'Merchant Navy' No 35015 *Rotterdam Lloyd* in the dark blue carried briefly and with some panache by the most powerful passenger engines, about to depart from Bournemouth West with the Waterloo-bound all-Pullman 'Bournemouth Belle' in the summer of 1951.
S. C. Townroe/Colour-Rail

Just back from overhaul at Eastleigh, 'M7' 0-4-4T No 51 is spotless – chimney and smokebox excepting – in olive green at Bournemouth shed, a few days before the outbreak of war in the summer of 1939. No 51 would survive until September 1962, a career spanning 57 years. *S. C. Townroe/Colour-Rail*

BR Standard '4MT' 2-6-0 No 76008 stands in Bournemouth Central with a stopping train from Weymouth, the rear carriage recently repainted in blue and grey, 8 April 1967. *R. C. Riley*

▲

In the latter days of main line steam operation over Southern
Region metals, a number of specials were operated using
locomotives from other regions. On 3 June 1967 the preserved
'A4' Pacific No 4498 *Sir Nigel Gresley* hauled one of these
specials; the locomotive is seen entering Bournemouth with the
return working. *R. C. Riley*

The old and the new orders pictured at Bournemouth Central
on 8 April 1967: the old is represented by BR Standard Class 4
2-6-0 No 76009 whilst the new appears in the sleek form of
Class 4-REP No 3003. *R. C. Riley*

▶

▲ Rebuilt 'Merchant Navy' No 35023 *Holland-Afrika Line* near
Sherborne with an up West of England express, 10 July 1959.
R. C. Riley

During the brief period after the first phase of the Kent Coast
electrification in June 1959, when members of the 'Schools'
class returned to the Western Section, No 30903 *Charterhouse* is
seen approaching Sherborne with a down Yeovil train, 30 July
1959. *R. C. Riley*

THE NATIONALISED YEARS

Nationalisation left Dorset seemingly at first unchanged, divided between the Western and Southern Regions, but this was a false lull, for the first dramatic change came on 2 April 1950. On that day the former Great Western main line to Weymouth south of Sparkford, the first station out of Castle Cary, passed to the Southern Region. Motive power and carriages continued to be largely ex-Great Western, and Great Western lower quadrant semaphore signals remained long after steam disappeared – indeed they have not entirely gone even as I write in the spring of 1998 – but Southern green gradually became the colour of stations. Great Western green became the livery of all larger BR passenger engines – after the 'Merchant Navies' had spent a short time in a handsome shade of blue – and black, with or without lining, for all the others. Corridor carriages became carmine and cream (or 'blood and custard' if you preferred), the rest dark red, although the Southern took a very long time to get rid of its green and in many instances never did – it was allowed to revert to green in the late 1950s.

Much greater changes were on their way. Being a deeply rural county, most of the branch lines of Dorset had never been exactly stretched to capacity, certainly outside the brief six weeks of the school summer holidays, and with the ever increasing prosperity of postwar Britain, car ownership increased rapidly. The first closure, a minor one, had been that of the spur between Corfe Mullen and Wimborne, way back in 1920 for passengers, 13 years later for goods. More significantly the Abbotsbury branch closed on 1 December 1952. Virtually all traffic in and out of this ancient and historic settlement a mile or so inland from Chesil Beach was in the direction of either Weymouth or Bridport. The railway to Weymouth followed a fairly roundabout route by way of Upwey Junction, while going by train to Bridport was even more so, involving two changes. Although a bus was offered as replacement this service faded away, so that today buses are as rare in

Abbotsbury as swans are commonplace. The attractive stone station at Abbotsbury became a residence. Goods traffic continued to use the short section between Upwey Junction and Upwey until 1962.

Despite the presence of the Royal and other navies, regular passenger services on the Portland branch, which had been worked by both the Southern and the Western, ceased on 3 March 1952. Passenger specials, including royal ones, and freight continued for more than a decade until the branch closed completely on 5 April 1965.

Away from the coast the Salisbury to West Moors line closed on 9 September 1963, bringing to an end through services between Wiltshire's cathedral city and Poole and Bournemouth. The line had been little used in later years, and never all that much throughout its career, which I

◀◀ The Abbotsbury branch was a relatively early casualty, being closed on 1 December 1952. Some six years later, on 24 July 1958, the intermediate station at Portesham is still remarkably intact – notice that even the cast sign on the left has survived; the only things lacking are traffic and track. The Abbotsbury branch, never one of the most commercially successful in the county, was opened on 9 November 1895 and absorbed by the Great Western in 1896. *R. C. Riley*

◀ With closure of the Abbotsbury branch Upwey Junction became Upwey & Broadway. In this 1979 picture the Great Western Society's train of vintage carriages resplendent in GWR livery passes through the station. The trackbed of the Abbotsbury branch can be seen to the right. *M. H. C. Baker*

have always found rather surprising, for plenty of people
have always travelled that way. In my student days in 1963
I hitch-hiked from Salisbury to Poole one summer
Saturday and found a vast amount of road traffic taking
this route.

Less than a year later on 2 May 1964 the whole of the
route from Brockenhurst through Ringwood and
Broadstone to Poole and Hamworthy Junction closed to
through traffic. Once the main line linking Dorset with
Southampton and London, it had lost much of its
importance but still carried a certain amount of goods and
passenger traffic, and was a very useful diversionary route
in the summer which enabled through trains to and from
Weymouth and Swanage to avoid Poole and Bournemouth.
The line from Wimborne remained open for freight a while
longer, which enabled the Queen to use the station for a
royal visit in July 1969.

One can argue that some of the closures were probably
justified but that of Castleman's Corkscrew was a serious
mistake for which the conurbation of Poole, Bournemouth
and Christchurch is now paying the price. Because so
much of the population lives far away from the one line
which serves it, the amount of rail commuter traffic it
generates is laughably minimal and nothing short of an
environmental disaster. Ringwood, West Moors, Wimborne,
Broadstone and Corfe Mullen have grown enormously
since the early 1960s, becoming in effect part of the
conurbation. If they were still served by the railway, traffic
congestion on the roads would be significantly less. The
fact that the track through Broadstone to Wimborne lasted
until not much more than 20 years ago and was then
ripped up says much about successive governments'
surrender to the road lobby. A road now occupies much of
the trackbed between Poole and Broadstone.

In the far west the Lyme Regis branch closed on 29 November 1965. In its final years a replacement had at last been found for the venerable Adams tanks in the shape of LMS-type Class 2 2-6-2Ts which took over in 1961. At a time when branch lines were closing all over the BR network the Lyme Regis closure attracted a certain amount of national attention but much more was focused on the county the following year, for on 7 March 1966 the whole of the Somerset & Dorset was abandoned. It had been in decline throughout the 1960s, the 'Pines Express' being diverted by way of Southampton and Oxford at the end of the 1962 summer timetable, and freight was also sent off elsewhere. The Western Region assumed control of much of the route and consequently such typically Swindon designs as '2251' 0-6-0s and pannier tanks appeared towards the end. Despite the publicity and the continuing nostalgia for the Somerset & Dorset, its loss is actually a good deal less significant than that of the Ringwood to Poole line.

By 1966 steam was getting very close to extinction on British Rail. Dorchester shed had shut, the Southern Region transferring its engines to Weymouth, where the Western presence was now no more. On the Waterloo to Weymouth main line many old favourites had gone, the last Drummond 4-4-0 in 1961, and the 'Schools' and 'King Arthur' classes were all withdrawn by the end of 1962, as was the last 'Lord Nelson', a class which had been concentrated on this line for many years. The 'M7s' lingered on for a little while longer, continuing to work from Bournemouth shed on the Swanage branch into 1964. The last nine members of the class were withdrawn from Bournemouth shed when the Ringwood line closed in May 1964. This meant Bulleid Pacifics and BR Standard designs now worked practically all services – a handful of

Maunsell 'S15' 4-6-0s and 2-6-0s lasted into 1966. Time was running out now even for the Pacifics, the first unrebuilt examples of the 'West Countries' and 'Battle of Britains' going in 1963, being followed shortly by the first rebuilt ones. The 'Merchant Navy' class began to be withdrawn in February 1964. Electrification and dieselisation elsewhere on the Southern meant that there were Pacifics to spare, so even a minor fault resulted in withdrawal.

On the Western decline in every respect was the order of the day. Slip coaches had remained as a curious relic of a practice once quite common, the last one to Weymouth, detached from the 3.30pm out of Paddington at Heywood Road Junction, Westbury, finishing in January 1959. Later

that year on 26 September, all through trains over the old GWR line from Weymouth to Paddington ceased. No 7010 *Avondale Castle* had charge of the last Paddington-bound boat train. This celebrated class was now going to the scrap-heap; diesel locomotives and railcars were taking over from steam on the Western line, although it would last into the mid-1960s. GWR '1366' class pannier tanks continued to work the Weymouth Quay branch even after an 'O3' class diesel took up work in April 1961, but they had all gone by 1964. With the ending of through Western Region services to London, much of the line between Dorchester, Yeovil Pen Mill and Castle Cary was singled in the mid-1960s.

On the narrow gauge lines serving the various clay

workings in the Isle of Purbeck steam had given way to diesel in the 1950s, but on the BR Swanage branch, which connected with the clay lines at Norden, beneath the towering ruins of Corfe Castle, steam survived the withdrawal of the 'M7s', with Ivatt LMS-type 2-6-2Ts and, notably, BR Standard 2-6-4Ts continuing until the autumn of 1966. DEMUs ousted steam from this date, but even then steam clung on for a little while longer, the daily clay train to and from Furzebrook often being steam-hauled, sometimes by a Pacific. These were mostly in a filthy, uncared-for state, often bereft of nameplates.

In September 1964 the electrification of the Waterloo to Bournemouth line was announced. The service would be operated by multiple-units. Beyond Bournemouth Central (Bournemouth West would be closed) Class 33 diesel-electric locomotives would take charge of one or, on some

journeys, two of the four-car trailer units which would stop at all stations to Poole, Wareham, Dorchester South and Weymouth.

The final day of steam on the Weymouth line was 9 July 1967. Although billed as the last steam main line, an increasing number of trains had already been handed over to either diesel or electric haulage. However the Channel Islands Boat Train continued to be steam-hauled until the end, as did the 18.15 Weymouth to Waterloo. The last regular steam-hauled down service was the 08.30 Waterloo to Weymouth on 8 July, in the charge of 'Merchant Navy' No 35023, while on the very last day the last steam-hauled train out of Weymouth was the 14.11 to Waterloo, hauled by 'Merchant Navy' No 35030, deputising for a failed Brush Type 4 (Class 47) diesel-electric locomotive.

And that was it. The final withdrawn steam engines

▶ Rebuilt 'West Country' No 34093 *Saunton* between Bincombe and Upwey tunnels with a Weymouth express, 23 July 1960. *Derek Cross*

were assembled at Salisbury and Weymouth sheds and hauled off to South Wales scrapyards. It was fortunate that many went to Woodham's yard at Barry for they were left there, in some cases for many years, giving the preservationists time to organise themselves so that a large proportion is still with us, many restored to active life. In Dorset steam has occasionally been seen on the main line, on both the former Western and Southern routes into Weymouth, but its greatest triumph has been on the Swanage Railway. After much work, both behind the scenes in persuading reluctant county councils and other parties, as well as visible physical progress, the first steam train for 12 years left Swanage station carrying fare-paying members of the public a few hundred yards along the relaid tracks on 5 August 1979. Today it is one of Britain's premier steam lines, carrying tens of thousands of passengers each year in the charge of, as in years gone by, representatives of BR Standard Class 4 tank, Bulleid Pacific and 'M7' 0-4-4T classes.

Rebuilt 'Merchant Navy' No 35007 *Aberdeen Commonwealth* speeds past Worgret Junction, west of Wareham, on 18 May 1966 with the 08.30 Waterloo to Weymouth. The branch line to Swanage diverges to the right. *C. W. R. Bowman*

'M7' 0-4-4T No 30059 crosses the viaduct over the Studland road immediately north of Corfe Castle, with a push-pull train of two LSWR carriages on a Swanage-Wareham working, c1953.
R. H. Tunstall

By 1961 Converted Maunsell push-pull units had replaced the LSWR ones. Another 'M7' has charge of one of these units, with a strengthening LSWR carriage immediately behind the engine, as it approaches Corfe Castle from Swanage in the summer of 1961.
J. E. Martin/G. B. J. collection

Bob Richards opens the level crossing gates at Wareham. Nowadays road traffic is carried by a flyover and the passenger crossing is controlled automatically. Bob Richards was the last regular signalman at Corfe Castle station in BR days. *M. H. C. Baker*

Hamworthy Junction *c*1959. A BR Standard '4MT' 2-6-0 stands at the island platform. *R. C. Riley*

In the last few years of the line's existence, the Western Region assumed control of the Somerset & Dorset, hence the appearance of Swindon-built '2251' class 0-6-0 No 3218 leaving Poole with a pick-up goods on a wet June day in 1965. *R. A. Panting*

◄◄ Far and away the most powerful engines ever to work over the S&D were the Riddles '9F' 2-10-0s. Being remarkably speedy for such small-wheeled engines, they were absolutely ideal. No 92006 sets off from Bournemouth West with the 3.40pm to Bristol, a featherweight load of four Maunsell corridors, in August 1961. *R. Puntis*

◄ For a period in 1953 when there was a problem with shifting driving wheels on the Bulleid Pacifics, a number of locomotives from the London Midland and Eastern Regions were drafted in to fill the gap. Gresley 'V2' 2-6-2 No 60893 is departing from Bournemouth Central with the 'Bournemouth Belle', 30 May 1953. *R. C. Riley*

◄ The 'S15' mixed-traffic 4-6-0s were regularly seen on stopping trains on the West of England main line. Here one of the Maunsell engines, No 30827 of 1927, pauses at Crewkerne with a five-coach up train, 26 July 1958. *R. C. Riley*